Watching While Waiting

Surviving the Pandemic Through Creativity and Reflective Practice

BONNIE ABADIE

Interior Image Credit: Bonnie Abadie

Library of Congress Control Number: 2025900724

ISBN: 979-8-90301-178-0 (sc)
ISBN: 979-8-90301-179-7 (hc)
ISBN: 979-8-90301-180-3 (e)

THE EWINGS PUBLISHING

One Galleria Blvd., Suite 1900, Metairie, LA 70001
(504) 702-6708

Contents

Part 1: Color Collection

Part 2: COVID Musings

Foreword

Cary Clack, Columnist, San Antonio Express News

"I know not everyone is comfortable with solitude," writes Bonnie Abadie in this beautiful and inspiring book you're holding in your hands. "Not everyone is able to sit still and reflect."

Bountiful is our gratitude that Bonnie isn't one of those people or we'd have been denied this sunbeam of creation which emerged from the darkness of COVID and lockdown. Without her ability to be still, to observe, think, feel, and write, our lives wouldn't be enriched with this gift of the spirit, this sharing of her soul.

"Watching While Waiting: Surviving the Pandemic through Creativity and Reflective Practice" is a collection of poems, reflections, paintings, and pictures which are, both, reportorial musings of what we endured during the pandemic but, also, meditations on joy and pain; love and grief; laughter and tears; loneliness and community.

It is a celebration of attentiveness, of looking inward at ourselves, and outward, at the world beyond. The better we understand and can connect to who we are, individually, the better we are able to understand and connect with the larger world animated by people, animals, and nature.

Anyone who has ever heard Bonnie sing knows of her gifts as a singer and musician. Her lyricism, voice, and sense of rhythm and melody translate, also, to the page.

One of the special things which Bonnie does in *"Watching While Waiting"* is turn her poetic gaze and inquisitive mind to the mysteries and meaning of colors and how each one contributes to the world's beauty and effects our mood, be they blue or grey, peach or green, barren brown, beautiful black, or moonlight white.

In *"Colors"* she writes:

> *Colors will teach us what we need to know*
> *Life, Love, Longing*
> *Pain, Passion, Possession*
> *Grief, Giving, Growing*
> *Letting Go*
> *Dying and Rising*
> *Colors of Life!*

Bonnie's writing, like how she lives her life, is shaped by her Roman Catholic faith but her writing, like her spirit, is transcendent, inviting, inclusive.

In *"Pathway to Peace"* she reminds us:

> *Peace comes at a price*
> *She demands your very life*
> *Be committed to her above all strife*
> *Peace is more than a starry night or*
>   *A majestic bird in flight*
> *Peace is the daughter of struggle*
>   *Serious struggle*

This broken world and the heartbreak in our lives can crush us. Bonnie acknowledges this pain.

But in this slim, yet essential volume of artistry, playful and prayerful she asks us to not ignore the beauty coursing through our lives and this world.

Beauty and love are abundant and waiting to be embraced. Watch for it.

Introduction

If you are reading this book in the 2020's, then you have survived some of the craziest and most difficult days of this century so far!

Who would have believed that with all our advanced medical knowledge and technologies, the world would be basically shut down by a microscopic virus known as the corona virus or COVID 19?!? And yet, it was. Millions of people died. Many millions more are affected by what is known as "long COVID".

Nothing made sense! When we feel sick, we go to the Doctor. At this time, the Doctors' offices had signs on them, "If you are feeling sick, do not come in. Go home and call 911."

Churches are places where we find spiritual strength and solace in grief. But at this time, churches were not places of refuge to the general public, they were allowing only 10 persons at a time.

Family is where we go when things are uncertain. But the lockdown insisted, "If you don't live there, you don't belong there. Go to your own residence and stay there until the lockdown is lifted."

People were acting strangely. I was fascinated by the toilet paper hoarding. As I watched this phenomenon, I wondered how toilet paper was expected to keep us safe from COVID.

After being told for years that too much alcohol was bad for us, I found it strange that liquor stores were open and experiencing booming success in sales.

Taken completely off guard, the citizens of the world were locked down, waiting for the pandemic storm to pass, watching ourselves in the process.

How did you weather this storm? Did you think the end of the world had arrived? Were you frightened and anxious? Were you able to greet each day with hope? Did you use the time for reflection and prayer? Did you explode in anger? Did you follow all the conspiracy theories? Were you caught in the political divide of pro and anti-vaccinations? Of masks and anti-masking debates? Did you suffer from depression? Did you lose a loved one to the dreaded virus? Did you contact the virus and arise victorious from its infection?

Did you participate in protests following the murder of George Floyd? Were you affected by riots and violence? Did you engage in conversations about race and racism in our country? Did you take up reading as a regular practice? Did you complete another academic degree? Did you use the time for catching up on projects around the home that had been previously put off? Did you find new hobbies and interests? Did you keep a journal of thoughts about the unfolding events?

Each of us had our own coping mechanisms. Aristotle, the great Greek philosopher once said, “the unexamined life is not worth living.” We certainly did a lot of waiting and watching. We waited for the development of safe vaccines and we watched how humanity responded to serious crises. The title of this book: *Watching While Waiting: Surviving the Pandemic through Creativity and Reflective Practice* issues an invitation to you, the reader, to take a moment, breathe deeply and reflect back upon our collective experience.

Reflective practice consists of taking time to examine the events in our lives and our responses to them. It is taking stock of our own lives and asking the question, "Where is God in all of this?" The lockdown seemed to be a forced time of retreat. It gave us a chance to look deeply at our lives, our habits, the things we take for granted. I appreciated the time in solitude as an opportunity for introspection. It allowed me time and space to appreciate how my life had taken on feverish activity; see my carbon footprint; understand the fragility of life itself. The lockdown helped me to see society in different ways. It gave me the chance to take off my blinders and be clear about the need for continuing human progress to end discrimination and racism. Most of all, the lockdown helped me to remember my relationship with and dependence upon God. I am not the creator of life! I do not sustain myself by myself.

I know not everyone is comfortable with solitude. Not everyone is able to sit still and reflect. As humans, we are by nature, social beings. We require and crave human contact. In this year of 2024, it seems to me that we are now caught up in collective amnesia. Having come through the roughest days, we seem to have forgotten what those lockdown days were like. Perhaps it is the brain's way of healing and of leading us toward the future.

Maybe we all want to put the painful past behind us. But, we learned valuable lessons that must be carried forward. What good are our experiences if we fail to learn from them? This is the reason why I decided to publish this collection of reflections, poems and musings: to share a glimpse of my own journey through COVID 19 lockdowns and to shine a light of hope into the future.

My first book, *Believing While Grieving: A Journey to Find Blessing in Brokenness*, published in 2019, and dedicated to my late husband, Maurice, was an offering of poems and pictures representing the journey through the loss of loved ones. Readers responded that my ability to name the places of pain and consolation were very helpful and spoke resoundingly to their experience. Because the feedback was so positive, I offer this work in that same spirit.

This book has two sections. The first section I call "Color Collection". In light of the keen awareness of color differences in people, these are playful conversations with various colors. Listen to what they reveal about life.

The second section I refer to as "COVID musings". These are a few prayerful reflections about life in that present moment. My faith background is Judeo-Christian, specifically, Roman Catholic, so these reflections are definitely tied to this orientation. It is my hope that there is a universal appeal that is inclusive and respectful of all people, all faiths, all backgrounds.

Accompanying each poem, reflection or musing is a piece of art or photo to help capture an aspect of the sentiments expressed. The artwork is offered as an additional invitation to reflect and pray. Art lovers appreciate its power to speak sometimes louder than words. These are all my "creations". I hope you will find them helpful in your journey toward understanding, acceptance and peace. Thank you for choosing this book!

Bonnie Lemelle Abadie, D Min.

Acknowledgements

This work would not be possible without the love and support of family and friends. Special **thanks** to all members of my family of origin: Patrick, Jules, Allen, Angela; their spouses: Olivia, Mary, Tim; nieces and nephews and all connected to: Marcel, Pua, Moreau, Alexis. To my New Orleans family: Johnnie and TJ, Yvonne, Rene and Cecelia; their offspring and all connected to Paul, Marie, Bryan, Dominic, David. To my "Formation House Family"—the Redemptorist Formation Community who adopted me as "Auntie" during COVID: Alipio, Antonio, Brian, Freddy, Huyen, Huan, Ivan, Jose, Peter, Royce, Ryan, Song, Steven, Thien. Thank you to my back porch company: Alipio, Antonio, Carmen, Caitlyn, Gloria, Huan, Ivan, Jennifer, Peter, Royce, Ryan, Sofia, Steven. Thank you also to the members of my COVID virtual communities: Sally, Theresa, Lizette, Jackie, Virginia, Lori, Ana Maria, Ana, Anne, Loraine and Graciela. Also to Dianne and the members of our weekly Centering Prayer group.

Heart-felt thank you to Cary for writing the foreword; to my readers: Helen, Jeannette, Karen, Peter and Rosie. I appreciate your participation in this project!

Thank you to the people from Balboa Press for making this work become a reality and thank you to Isaura for introducing me to them.

Finally, thanks to the members of my faith community, St. Gerard Catholic Church for keeping me grounded and to my friends and colleagues at the Oblate School of Theology for keeping me moving forward.

Dedication

This book is lovingly dedicated to all who were affected by COVID 19, especially those who died and those who mourn their passing.

To all of our pandemic heroes:

The members of the medical profession who gave their tireless and best efforts to fight COVID, preserve life, and provide comfort to the patients and their families.

The essential employees who risked their lives to provide services, food, medicine and supplies for everyone.

The teachers who valiantly rose to new heights of creativity to educate our young people.

Part 1

Color Collection

Colors

Swirling, twirling, dancing, unfurling
Blessings within
Blessings above
Blessings below
Blessings abroad
Colors brilliant, muted, vibrant, dark
All are gift
All can receive
All is Well
Places in the heart
Tattered, battered, beleaguered
Born again in the baptism
Water, Spirit, Earth, Air, Fire
Breath, movement and desire
Shine, dance, be still, observe
Colors will teach us what we need to know
Life, Love, Longing
Pain, Passion, Possession
Grief, Giving, Growing
Letting Go
Dying and Rising
Colors of Life!

Blue and Grey

Blue and Grey the sky today
	Sunshine and Rain dance together again
Blue and Grey my soul today
	Caught in the web of grief, looking for relief
Blue and Grey my heart today
	Torn between the future and the past
	Torment that lingers and lasts
Blue and Grey my time today
	Looking for hope in despair
	Finding light and air.
Blue and Grey my thoughts today
	Tangled in riddles and rhymes
	Walk with me through time
Blue and Grey our world today
	What is truth? What are lies?
	Look up!
We are called to rise!

Just Peachy

Not the innocence of pink
Not the boldness of orange
But a combination of the two
Peach blossoms playfully in a new land
Open to freshness and new beginnings
Peach recalls the promise of Vibrance
Commands the respect of darker hues
Stands in the threshold and beckons
Come see the place where hope is born
Come behold my colors at dawn
Come see the brilliance of being born
        of two realities
        joined in passionate embrace
Pink and orange
Morning light, show how everything about which I
        Worry and scurry
        Will turn out
        Just Peachy!

Purple

The color of Advent, the time of my birth
The color of Lent, the time to repent
        and be converted to the Gospel
Purple for waiting has more blue
Purple for Passion has more red
What color purple speaks best to you?
Purple, the color of suffering and ecstasy
Purple, the color of wisdom and pain
Purple that fashions us to rise again
Purple, the color of this state I'm in
        Funky, fuzzy, hazy
        Fusion of energetic and lazy
Purple has no pretense
Let her fill the nights and days of your new beginning
Notice the light
        dancing off the bi-colored threads
        of surrender and resistance
Purple calls us to watch for the dawn!
Purple is the color of encounter
Emerging out of grey
Purple issuing a new day
Profoundly **u**niting **r**eal **p**eople **l**iving **e**verywhere!

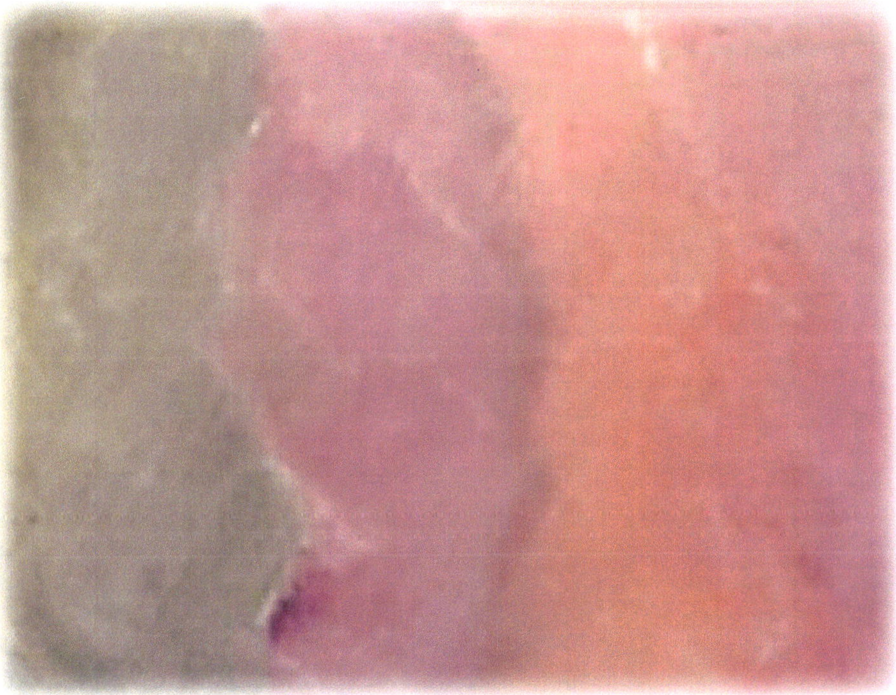

Moonlight White

Full Moon of late Summer
Lazily sweeping across the Western Sky
Bright white light creasing shadows in the night
What kind of fool stays up to watch this brilliance?
One fool looking for resilience!
Staring at the moon makes life timeless
I revisit August nights of my childhood
When I exchanged loving glances with the smiling moon
Wondering if it was really made of cheese?
How did it get there?
Was the man in the moon eating it all up?
I remember a moonlit night of my adolescence
When the pain of growing up
Had me secretly planning my escape to New York City
Where I would be free of parental tyranny!
Moon's white light saved me from being a runaway.
And I gave my life to Jesus in the brilliance of that night.
A few more moons and I was all grown up!
Clear memory has me reliving moonlit walks with my Beloved
In places where only the moon could see us
Only her white light could find us
This beautiful moon that laser-cut our hearts
And soldered them together
This bright white light that revealed the face of love

And ignited passion leading to unity and ecstasy
The sweetness of the Honey Moon I can touch
And taste again in this light.
So, yes, it's nearly two a.m., but what is time in eternity?
The bright white light of Sister Moon
    calls and recalls
    shines and refines
    reveals and heals the cracks of time
White Full Moon brilliance I am glad to see
White Full Moon brilliance I am called to be.

Lavender

Not quite pink and not quite purple,
Lavender dwells in the border lands
Calm presence begging to be noticed
Beckoning all who will listen
To her silent whisper
But she never whimpers,
Lavender has lots to say:
I am bold but beautiful
I am sweet but I am strong
When you come nearer you
Can hear my song
Mixture of lullaby and laughter
Bringing tranquility and rapture
Be still for a moment and capture
The essence of Lavender found in your soul.
Sweet strength, bold essence
Calm and tranquil
I obey the call to stop
And notice.

Turquoise

Blue of Sky
Green of Earth
Melding into true companionship
Turquoise, the color of fidelity
The stone my Beloved loved to give me.
Blue of Sea
Green of Algae
Dancing together as they belong
Notes of a hopeful love song
Turquoise smiles as though she knows
Where the time goes!
Blue of Dusk
Green of Twilight
Day of delight comes to rest
Bringing sorrow to my breast
Turquoise stands in witness of all that has been.
Blue of night
Green of stars twinkling above
Dark is dark and pain is stark
Turquoise knows it is not the end
Faithfulness is eternal
Place your sorrows on the wind
Blue of sadness

Green of hope
Mingle together with time and pressure
Turquoise the rock life does measure
Upon this rock I have hung my heart
How do I start to:

Breathe again
Love again
Dance again

Turquoise will teach me how
It is the color of now!

Beautiful Black

Darkest darkness, stark absence of light
Black is classic simplicity
Strongest before the crack of dawn where your boldness waits
        to greet me in a coffee cup
You nestle in places where hope dares to find you!
Beautiful Black, the color of skin that makes other colors afraid
You matter most certainly and most of all!
Patience incarnate, absorbing all heat
Black, the shadow present in endless day
Framer of fairer colors
Home to silence and secret
You compliment and accompany
        All who seek Truth
Preparing the soul to receive the Light
Black of night, absence of light
Hide me within the folds of your darkest darkness
The home of eternal peace.

Marvelous Midnight

Stroke of which changes everything
Mysterious and Magnificent
Midnight, you are the shade of blue
        That makes dreams come true
Fairy-tale obscurity, you hold most certainly
        The soon-to-be-revealed happy ending
But, not so fast! Don't kid yourself,
Midnight hides the path
Darkness most deep casts the mantle
Where sleep draws forth uncertainty
Lost in the folds of your garment
No light to guide, no flicker to shine
Midnight and madness combine to confuse
        And refuse false hope.
Marvelous Midnight, my resting place
Confound the rush to resurrection
Until in your grace,
Morning breaks!

Gregarious Green

Spring and sage, shamrock
and shades of Summer's Pasture
You invite us to cast our cares into the forest
and emerge renewed.
Green, you are the most seen color on Earth
How is it that you are both the color
Of potential and envy?
The color of greed and money,
You are also the color of serenity and hope!
Emerald, Olive, Avocado, Spinach, Collard, Mustard and Algae
Green, with your many nurturing incarnations,
Spring forth from the mouth of God
Fill the Earth with budding, emerging celebrations of promise
And awaken life itself
    In our darkened hearts!

Barren Brown

Dirt, dust, Earth, musk,
bark, mulch and sand.
Brown, you are the color by which we get down
    To humility and the restoration of
    All that is simple
    All that is true
Barren Brown, we can all believe in you
We are all marked by your brush!
Hair, eyes, skin striking fear in the hearts of those
    Who think they are going extinct
Brown boldly colors the birds of the sky, the question, "why?"
Brown brings us down to earthiness
Where the soul returns to its Creator
    And the body to dust
Achievements and accolades mellow into rust
Brown receives and celebrates us all!

Tangerine

No ordinary Orange,
Tangerine combines the beauty of red
        And the sassiness of sunset
Mixing and melding into a celestial shade
        Surpassing either color alone.
Tangerine, like a tambourine
        Beats rhythms of salsa and cumbia and tango
She is sexy and sensual!
How are you going to celebrate her invitation,
to shake off the shackles of
        dreariness and boredom?
When will you surrender to the
        Laughter that shakes the walls
        Of your carefully crafted fortress?
Feel the beat, let your soul retreat
Tangerine will take you
where you never thought you could go!

Bella Yellow

Beautiful, loud and boisterous, you are everywhere!
To greet us in the morning, you are there!
You are chasing away the blues,
No wonder I'm bananas about you!
Lemon, cornflower, muted shades of gold
Yellow breaks and bellows through boredom
And reveals the life waiting outside
    The Empty Tomb!
The color of warmth and joy,
You steal through the cracks in the gray walls
    Surrounding my soul
You stay, inviting me to play
    In the sunshine of ecstasy
You want to be the flame that ignites the light
    Of hope in the Human Spirit
Welcome, Yellow! Come do your Thing!

Azure

The color of leisure
The invitation of swimming pools
    And playful oceans
    And cloudless skies
Azure is there to assure
    Life is precious
    Time can't wait
Blue caress of infinite rest
Bring me to tranquility
Let my anxious heart see
    The calm that prevails
May all our travails
    Fade into Azure blueness.

Scarlet

Rising from the primary palate
You give birth to all the shades of red
On the horizon at sunset you inspire
    Artists and poets
    Friends and lovers
On the blade of a knife or a bullet torn through flesh
You are the color of life itself.
On the interior landscape you are
    The color of love and passion,
But also of fear, violence, anger and rage
Yet, Scarlet you are faithful in every age.
In a Black and White world
You call us to awaken to a life beyond boredom
    And humdrum
Scarlet is the sentinel and herald of vibrant potential
Let us stop, listen to your song
    And dance to the new beat coming forth
From the Eternal Heart.

Find the Rainbow in the Rain

The colors of gloom, the starkness of pain
Abide for a while, but do not reign
Look for the light and look again
You'll find the rainbow in the rain
Colors soft and muted hide behind
          The humoral veil
Keep your eyes fixed to behold every detail
Colors of hope, passion, strength and love prevail
Darkness, the canvas for beauty without fail.
Walk in confidence with both feet
Though one wants to progress, the other retreat
Remember your purpose and once again
Find the rainbow in the rain.

Blue Black Butterfly

Where have you come from? Where are you going?
With grace that rocked my soul
You flit into my life
Lacing it with wonder and surprise
You captured my heart as you danced before my eyes

I didn't ask for you to come, but here, you found a home
I want to have you within my grasp
But will kill you with possessive clasp
For Love gives you wings
Fly and be free!

You may love me and leave me,
catch me on the rebound,
But let your laughter resound
Allow me to look, not capture
Love, not own
Admire, not desire.

I lift you up, I give you over
As you play in field of clover
While I shall be grateful for your appearance
Follow your flight pattern with delight

Trust the Purpose of God for your Life
Be it short or long
Your beauty forms a song
The melody survives

Where have you come from? Where are you going?
MYSTERY!
Take a little piece of me
Secure in Love's glance
Fly and be free!

The Red Tent of Providence

See, I spread the tent before you Marvelous red,
vibrant with all seasons of life.
A place of welcome and hospitality.
A home for souls weary of drudgery.
Come enter this dark, quiet, mysterious portal
and behold my presence in the smiles of your sisters
in the warm embraces of love
in the holy places housing mirth in the room,
this womb of rebirth.
Let me provide for you
as you strive to be light and salt and city on the hill.
Come drink your fill of abundantly flowing wine.
Lay down your regrets of the past.
Your questions of the future.
Be nurtured in the NOW and know I Provide!

Part 2

COVID Musings

How am I doing?

I always say, "Fine, thank you."
But lately, my default response is, "I'm alive! It's a good day!"
I am grateful for the gift of life and the daily gift of potential and grace.
I am also still caught in the COVID fog.
The feeling of fatigue and listlessness even as I have demands waiting at my door,
piling up on the floor, these demands and more
the children of my "yeses" stand waiting for their turn.
I'm afraid some will be lost in the wilderness of what used to be my brain.
Watching the smoke from the incense flute dance near the candle flame,
there's fleeting shapes and forms.
They dance and are gone! A metaphor for life.
I see the split-second of beauty and have to capture the moment for joy.
Can't hold it for any longer than one tick of the second hand as it dissipates into
the air leaving a holy scent to follow in prayer.
How am I doing?
I'm running to keep up with myself who while seemingly in slow motion
is more active than I want to be.
I want to spend more quiet time to reflect.
I want to watch the birds and lizards and wild life, the circle of life in my back yard.
I want to stare and think of nothing in particular but everything in general.
I want to wait and hibernate.
Until the coast is clear
Until Corona breaks her crown

Until we can come down to take a safe vaccine
Until I regain the energy demands of the life I claim
I want to stake a permanent claim on my "Summer Home" and live there
"Happily ever after"
I want the philosophical discourse
The theological discussions
The political and social conversations
And nothing more!
But that doesn't bring an income, does it?
So I have to push past this desire and
Stay in the game!
That's how I'm doing.

The Back Porch

Simple space, not much to see,
    But it's been a "Summer Home" to me.
A table, three chairs, two fans, bug spray
    Fresh flowers to cheer the heart, wind chime with a fleur de lis.
A sanctuary and front row seat to
    Mother Nature's unlikely retreat:
My own back yard!
Morning coffee to greet the day in prayers
    Of gratitude and supplication for friends and our nation
Inspiration for new strength to grab hold of work
    Or endless meetings and classes on zoom
Fortified to testify that God is Good.
Evening greetings of gentle breezes and pop in visits
    From soul friends and favorite creature
Enchanted by party lights
    In the gathering twilight
Wine like conversation freely flowing
    Unpacking the news of the day:
Deadly COVID ravages, economic disasters,
    Protests, social unrest, Black Lives Mattering for real this time?

Grown up temper tantrums and other such people behaving badly
"We're all gonna die"! The common refrain.
Difficult and deep explorations of the roots of racism, colorism, gender
        Fearlessly asking and answering, "What is that like for you?"
Spending time in the others' shoes and
        Looking at life through different lenses.
Generous hospitality giving space to release
        Pent-up poison, unpacked baggage, rancid resentments
Released into the arms of the Redeemer.
Dreams alive and dreams denied
        Held by strong hands, protecting from abysmal chaos
Healing through judgement-free listening that understands.
Problems of Church and World suspended
        In this Summer moment of time
        In the safe and brave space of grace
        The Back Porch

COFFEE
TIME

Another Spin on the Wheel

Monday comes in a few hours
And ready or not, here is the new school year!"
Another spin on the wheel!
Beginning as we ended
Hidden away as best we can be
From the deadly virus we can't even see
Holding classes in the land of technology.
Sending students to minister in cyberspace
This world is so weird to me!
Still, I breathe and greet each moment
As it appears
Using my eyes and ears
I will continue to lead even as I follow
The direction set forth by the Good Shepherd.
My sheep have a new pasture
But I am still walking with the Master
Take my place on the wheel
As God gives us another spin!

Let Your Spirit Soar!

Open that door
You've been locked there in fear
    For way too long!
Life is a gift of flight
Let your spirit soar!
Receive the gifts I give
I want you to truly live
You are young in eternity
    Trust me
Let your spirit soar!
Tears are your river
    Don't stay on the bank
Enter the flow and go
    Where the water takes you
Let yourself go!
The wind blows the breath of the Spirit
Begin to unfurl your wings
Let your heart sing
Let your spirit soar!

South Texas Snowfall

Silent, Steady, Stealthy, Snowfall
Softly drifting, wind driven
Like powder, like ash
Reminder of the interplay of life and death
Stillness of breath
Behold the Mystery in each flake
Special, Sensational, Sacramental, Sacrificial
Behold it like an adult
It is bothersome and dangerous
Behold it like a child
It is magical and miraculous
Suffering while celebrating
Mesmerizing
Snow

To Have Known Love

I am so fortunate to have known love!
That crazy energy that shakes your world
    And turns you inside out and upside down
That kind of love that sees who you are
    And who you can become
That kind of love that holds you in good times and in bad
    In sickness and in health
That kind of love that leads you to places
    You never knew you could ever go
That kind of love that brings you
    To heights and depths and breadths and lengths
Of the upper-outer-inner-most
    stretches of the soul
That kind of love that helps you breathe
    And takes your breath away
That kind of love that faces all things together
    For as long as you are together
That kind of love that takes you through sunrises
    And to the ultimate sunset
Yes, I am fortunate to have known
    THAT kind of love
I am forever grateful!

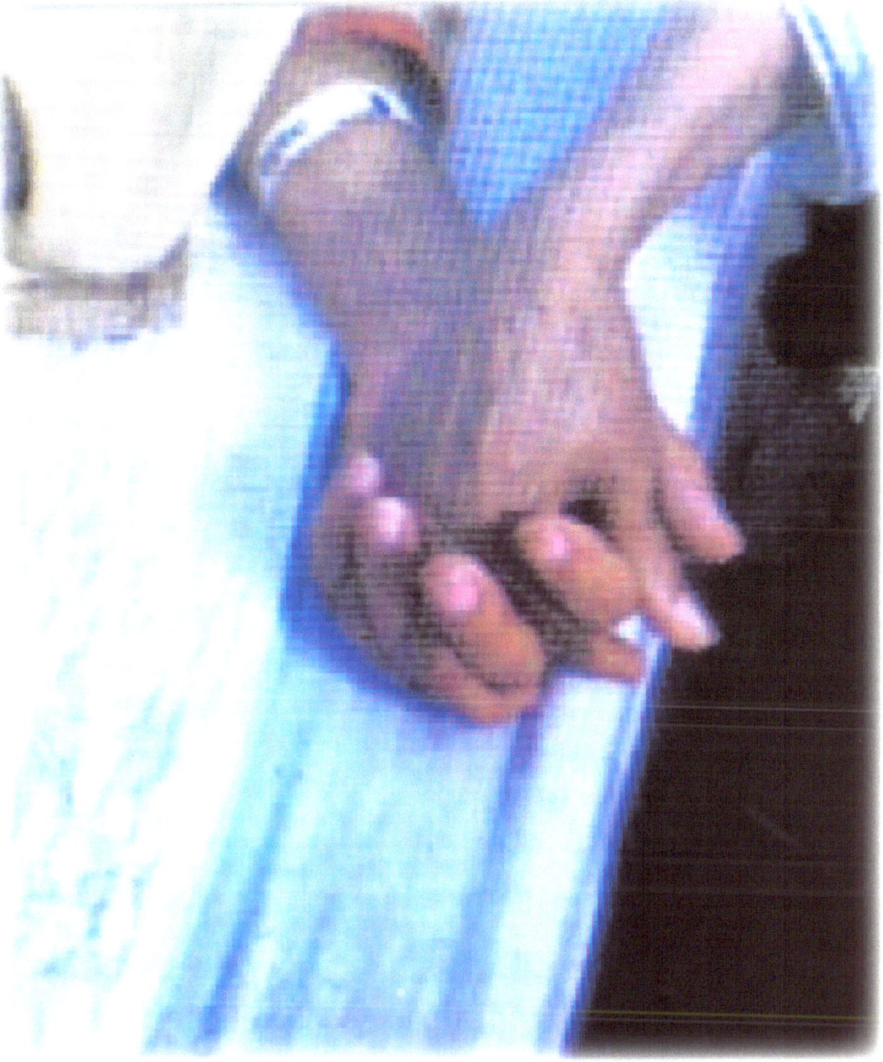

October Night

Flashes of white lightening eerily
Streaking across the black sky in brilliantly blinding display
Booming thunder crackling, shaking the windows
Vibrating the door and my floor
Powerful Mother Nature, are you here to play?
Purple rain falling heavily upon my roof
The stuff of horror movies
Moving in the real moment
October night, delightful fright
Change is once again in the air
Life giving way to death, mother nature losing her breath
But we know her secret!
Death is the door to new life we each must open
The corridor is long
Stretching the length of eternity
Darkness makes it hard to see
There is approaching dawn.

Last Day of November

Both warm and cool,
The day ambles in mist and fog
Issuing an invitation to retrospection
Falling leaves invite the inner child to dance
    And fall upon neatly raked piles
The joy of the crunch and the annoyance at the clutter
    Both tell me I am a paradoxical child of the earth
Called to both
    Delight and frustration
    Playfulness and seriousness
    Rejoicing and mourning
    Dancing and being still
Seeming contradictions are seen in clearer light
The invitation to life is not just black and white
Behold the brilliance of dying leaves against the stark grey sky
Joy against sorrow
Life against death
Winds of change, life's breath
"Soon there will be barren branches, tomorrow perhaps
But do not cease celebrating well your life today", says
This last day of November.

The Coming Winds of Change

Winds of change are coming
Gusty gales whirlwind swirling
Twirling and blowing the old away
Leaves that cling to not yet bare trees
Cannot resist the invitation to flee
So blow away all the rust and dust
Change skepticism to trust
Blow into each heart and soul
Swirl so that the broken becomes whole
Expectations cannot be forged
For all is in flux
The future cannot be seen
For all is possibility
Clinging to the past and the present
Is as useless as the clinging of leaves
And so we all must be blown
Wherever the Spirit leads
Take flight to new heights
Ride the coming winds of change.

Sofia Freed

Fitted for over a month with a most fashionable
        Pink, blue, black
        Psychedelic cone
Sofia, madly thrashing in the grass
        Snaps the chain that binds
The confinement is done
Sofia is Free!
Sofia, let your wisdom teach us that
        We too can snap the bonds of oppression
We too can emerge like you
Free!

Stirrings

Sitting in stillness
Songs of Angels by Hildegard stir my heart,
    Soul, mind and places deep within
    Leaving me breathless with wonder
Love notes bouncing in air stirring my whole self
    To compassionate embrace
    Of all that is known to God.
Embers of passion stirred into flame
    Brilliant in shades of red, orange, gold
Time between Ascension and Pentecost
    Wait for the Spirit our Christ will send
    Then we can spend our lives as wild
    and far-reaching Instruments
Notes of Ascension from Hildegard
Bringing joy, speaking peace, giving life
    Giving MY life
    Being Life itself in each moment
Stirrings in silence
Notes of praise by all that is loved by God

Keep Your Eyes on the Horizon

The light is fading, but it is not yet dark
Keep your eyes on the horizon
The Light of the World
Remains the spark
That sets creation ablaze
And reveals new ways
Of Truth, Joy and Peace.
Keep your eyes on the horizon
Remain calm and clear about
Who has REAL power here
If "Truth is not Truth",
Then all are covered in lies
Open your eyes and see
I am TRUTH beyond belief
Look to me and be not confused
By the fabricated chaos.
Keep your eyes on the horizon
Receive "Big Picture" Wisdom
Faith is tested, Joy arrested
Peace disturbed, souls perturbed
Troubles arise, Justice falls
God still calls us to be faithful!
Keep your eyes on the horizon.

Grateful

The joy of opening my eyes to another day
I greet God's time with an attitude that portrays gratitude
To be grateful, I realize
I must let go of anguish and anxiety
Allowing the breath of the Spirit to fill my heart
    With only goodness and peace
More than optimism, gratitude proclaims belief
    That God is truly in charge
My thanks unlock vistas wide with grace and wonder
Grateful is the spell I'm under
The chance to see how my worries
    make me no less ready to be in charge
    of what God has already claimed
Full of your goodness,
I am Grateful!

Pathway to Peace

Do not think there is a smooth Pathway to Peace
You must take the road that is rough and steep
Like many have taken before
Peace is to be sought and fought for
She is the inner spark of the Divine!
Peace comes at a price
She demands your very life
Be committed to her above all strife
Peace is more than a starry night or
    A majestic bird in flight
Peace is the daughter of struggle
    Serious struggle
She is the journey to the center of the heart
She is the pathway in the journey to the soul
Peace is the Presence of God
    That makes us whole
Peace commands my full attention
She is here, if I but listen
Let her settle, Let her dance
Let us finally give Peace a chance!

Be Tenacious

You've been in hard places before
One never knows what life has in store.
The tiny ivy growing in the mortar's crack
Invites one to see life in the present moment
And that against all odds,
In spite of all obstacles,
Grace grants what human wisdom lacks:
The audacity of tenacity!

You Are Worth More Than Many Sparrows

The flocks of sparrows that fill my backyard
Sing a constantly reminding refrain,
"God cares for us!"
"God cares even more for you!"
"We are worthy of God's love!"
"So are you!"
Fear not, little flock
You are known to God
You are held in God's embrace
Remember your worth in God's eyes
Small but mighty
Insignificant yet essential
Ordinary yet precious
Your little life gives glory to your Creator
Sing your song
Live your purpose.

Afterword

Dear Reader, thank you for allowing me to share part of my COVID journey in creativity and reflective practice with you. I hope you found places where our experiences connected and resonated. Life is a great, beautiful gift filled with joys and sorrows; tragedies and triumphs. As you look back over your own journey of waiting and watching through dangerous and difficult days, may you find consolation and peace in knowing you are not alone. As we continue to celebrate life, let us be grateful for the precious time we have been given!

About the Author

Bonnie Lemelle Abadie, D. Min., Associate Professor of Pastoral Studies at the Oblate School of Theology, is a native of San Antonio, Texas. Throughout her life in ministry (40+years) in the Roman Catholic Church, she has served as a teacher, facilitator, retreat director, catechist, liturgist, youth and young adult minister, campus minister, spiritual director, formation associate, conference speaker, singer and musician. She is an award-winning poet and fledgling artist.

What People Are Saying About This Book

Truly a beautiful and inspiring book.

—Cary Clack, San Antonio, Texas

I absolutely love the poetry, art and reflections in this new book.

—Jeannette Easley, Houston, Texas

This artistically written book is an eye opener to the beauty that surrounds us that we often take for granted. I love how Bonnie describes our colorful surroundings in nature, and also how colors play into everyday life. This book is a great reminder of the gratitude we owe to our God for having survived Covid, but also for the beautiful world in which we live.

—Rosie Flores, San Antonio, Texas

Bonnie's writings open me to feel, explore, confront, embrace, to consider, and celebrate life and God. What a wonderful journey, one I will return to many times.

—Karen Grossman, Portland, Oregon

I am thankful to have received a pre-publication copy. What a beautiful read! Bonnie's heart and soul are in every sentence. I've read it over and over again. Yes, it is about Covid, but it is also a beautiful love story woven throughout the poetry and art work.

—Helen Q. White, Syracuse, New York

www.ingramcontent.com/pod-product-compliance
Lightning Source LLC
LaVergne TN
LVHW070954210926
848482LV00002B/214
9798903011780